A Robin on my Tea Cup

A Country Calendar

By Vicky Turrell

Published by Leaf by Leaf Press Ltd 2017
www.leafbyleafpress.com

Copyright © Vicky Turrell 2017

Vicky Turrell has asserted her right to be identified as the
author of this work in accordance with the Copyright,
Design and Patents Act 1988

ISBN 978-0-9957154-4-8

Printed and bound in Great Britain by Clays Ltd, St Ives plc

The countryside in words and pictures
through the months.

Acknowledgements

I would like to thank Colin Channon the editor of the Oswestry and Borders Advertizer for his constant support and encouragement. The accounts in this book are taken from my regular Nature column in his excellent newspaper.

I would also like to thank members of the Oswestry Writing Group and the members of Leaf by Leaf Press for all their help. I am grateful to John Heap for his work in preparing my notes for publication.

My thanks also go to Greg Manterfield-Ivory for his help in preparing for the printing process by Clays.

Finally, I thank my family for showing their appreciation of my work.

'Every good local newspaper editor likes to have variety in their publications – from the hard news stories which readers still clamour for, to campaigns, to features and sport...and the occasional softer, far more gentle article.

The experts call it "changing the pace" of a newspaper- a fancy phrase, but oh so true.

Vicky Turrell's Nature column is that change of pace. After reading about the hurly burly of everyday life that can be found on the news pages, turning to Vicky's column is like a summer breeze gently smoothing out the stresses and strains.

Caterpillars, mushrooms, a lost hen, birds nesting where they shouldn't – who would have thought such subjects would transfix a reader?

Vicky writes with such knowledge and passion that it's easy to imagine you're on the farm beside her as she pens her column.

(I imagine she's tapping away at an old typewriter, with a glass of red at her elbow and her famous hat shielding her eyes from the sun that's slowly going down...)

Keep changing that pace Vicky. The Advertizer just wouldn't be the same without it.'

Colin Channon,
Editor of Oswestry and Borders Advertizer

January
The wayward waxwing

On a cold winter's day, a few years ago, I saw an unusual bird on our telephone wire. It was a pinkish colour and had a crest of feathers standing up on its head. Other birds were mobbing it. Their loud calls attracted my attention.

Eventually the bird escaped to the woodland and landed on a secluded guelder rose bush. It ate a few red berries before flying away into the sunset towards the town.

The next day it was back but this time it landed on our cotoneaster which was covered in bright berries. It began to devour them greedily and I watched from my bedroom window as it ate breakfast, lunch and dinner before flying off again into the setting sun. It repeated its activity for about a week. I was fascinated by this strange bird and noticed it had red tips to its wings and wondered if it had been hurt – perhaps by the other birds mobbing it. Was that blood on its wing? No, this was a waxwing and the red is part of its normal colouring. Its wings look as if they have been dipped in sealing wax.

We had sealing wax at home when I was a little girl and we played with the solid red stick, kept in my father's desk, melting it with a lighted match and watching the blood red drips.

Do you remember sealing wax? Important letters used to come in the post tied with string on the flap and sealed with red wax. There was usually an impressed stamp so you could be sure that the letter was secure. Nowadays we look for the lock sign on a web site to make sure our messages are safe. How times change.

That winter, a few years ago, I heard that a huge flock of waxwings was in town. But my waxwing had come alone to us and I wondered if, as it was flying over our garden it saw our berry trees. Then as the others flew on, my waxwing fell behind. Perhaps it thought, 'I will let the others go on ahead and I can drop down here and have the food all to myself,' it could have landed on our delicious food to feast undisturbed and unchallenged.

This year I have resorted to Twitter (where else would you look to find out about birds?) to see if anyone has noted them heading this way. On @WaxwingsUK you can find out where they are. In October, they were seen in the counties on the east coast. They flew over from Scandinavia across the North Sea in search of food and the Tweeters recorded yesterday that waxwings are coming west and are in North Wales. Every movement is reported.

We have a lot to look forward to in the New Year even if the weather turns cold because then, you may see waxwings. Look anywhere where there are berries in gardens or supermarket car parks. They are a treat to watch all together but if a greedy one sneaks away from the flock and comes alone to feast here on our berries, I won't report it. Its secret is safe with me, my lips will be sealed.

January
The endangered ash tree

One night recently I heard an almighty cra-a-a-ck like a firework going off in our field called Ash Patch. In the morning, I saw a huge broken branch, hanging dangerously from our ash tree. Was this the dreaded fungus causing 'ash die back'?

I wonder if you remember Dutch Elm disease when all our elm trees were wiped out. The unthinkable happened then and could happen again. We must look after our ash trees, I thought, before it's too late.

I called a tree surgeon and he came the next day. Wearing protective clothing, he scaled our mighty tree, roping himself on as he climbed. The branch was sawn off neatly and he left a pile of cut logs for our burner. They will give us a good steady heat next year.

'It is not ash die back,' said the tree surgeon, 'you would see tips of green shoots shrivelling, as well as die back at the top of the tree,' we breathed a sigh of relief. 'However, it is still in danger,' he added.

The hooting owl sits here at night amongst the black buds and this is where the squirrels play in the day under the filigree canopy. This is where the winter fieldfares congregate and where love doves sit in the summer cooing and kissing.

'How can we save our tree?' we asked. The tree surgeon suggested cutting the ivy away as it was making the branches heavy and could have caused this one to break. So, that is what we have done. Our ash tree is safe for the moment.

It is the second time our ash tree has been threatened. One day I came home to find that electricity poles were being erected near the tree. There was going to be a transformer slung between them and the tree branches were going to be cut to make way for the poles. I didn't know what to do. This was before Swampy dug tunnels and eco-warriors lived in trees to save the countryside and I had to go to work, so I left a feeble note, 'Do not cut this ash tree. Signed...' and then I crossed my fingers and hoped for the best.

This mighty ash took root in the hedgerow during WWI and then survived and grew through WWII. It would have seen horses pulling carts around Ash Patch. It would have seen families with growing children bursting through our front door. Then electricity and water came up the lane and the old well was covered over and paraffin lamps were thrown out. It survived freezing temperatures in 1963, the drought of 1976 and the gales of 1987. Now it was going to be cut down in the name of progress.

But somehow, the ash tree was not cut down and the poles and transformer were put up in a kind neighbour's field instead, away from any trees. Our ash was safe that time too.

Now I have heard that there is a third threat, the emerald ash borer beetle is about to come from Sweden and kill any surviving ash trees.

It seems that there is nothing we can do to save them this time, except perhaps cross our fingers, call for Swampy and touch wood (if there is any left).

February
The brave sparrows

Did you know that February 2nd is the birds' wedding day? When I first came to Shropshire the postman told me this and I am inclined to believe him because only a few days ago, I saw a house sparrow with a feather in its beak heading for our eves.

House sparrows are everywhere here in Shropshire and if you have a bird table, you will see them crowding round the food, they often force out the timid little birds and even the smart blackbird. House sparrows love seeds and today they are on our bird table making a great deal of noise and creating lots of mess. They seem to be just ordinary common birds, with not much to be said in their favour.

Last year, my husband was given a nest box with a camera fitted and he put it up on a tree trunk straight away. In our excitement, we didn't check the size of the hole (which had several adjustments) and we were disappointed that it was large enough for a pair of familiar house sparrows, who immediately claimed it.

You could connect the camera to the TV via a long cable which we pushed through our living room window. Soon we were watching from the comfort of our armchairs. We saw, on screen, the sparrows 'build' a messy nest inside the box. They took in dry grass to make a bundle then filled it with feathers. The female laid five white eggs and the birds took turns incubating. You could see the eggs clearly when one of the pair stood up to change shifts. After

12 days, they were proud parents and we felt that we were too.

The box had a microphone so we could hear the babies shouting for food when a parent darkened the hole to come in. We could see big orange gapes as the babies craned their necks to get an insect or a juicy caterpillar. We didn't get many jobs done that week, as we couldn't resist spying on the everyday life of two, suddenly interesting, brown birds.

Then, I don't know what went wrong, but one morning, when we turned on, one baby bird was dead. Then another died and another, there were only two left. Was it the wet summer? Was it the lack of food? We did not know the answer. We switched the screen off and couldn't bear to watch any more.

There seem to be thousands of house sparrows here in Shropshire but my sister in Yorkshire says that she hardly ever sees one these days. The RSPB will tell you that sparrows have declined rapidly in the last 30 years and could be in danger. These little birds used to be pests. They were as common as mice, raiding the corn field and crowding the roads to scavenge every grain dropped by the farmers' trailers. Now they are under threat.

So, look out for them this spring when all the birds dress up in their spring attire. You will see house sparrows in their new, smart brown outfits.

I hope they enjoy their wedding day, this Thursday. I will throw them some seeds and wish them good luck. These sociable, friendly, brave, happy little birds might not be here next year.

February
First flowers

The race for survival has begun in the countryside. First the winter aconite hastened to flower under our hedge. You can see the bright yellow blobs from our window, pushing up through the dead leaves. Nothing deters them – even snow will not stop their lamp-like glow. They seize the opportunity before ruthless spring plants grow and crowd them out.

You don't see many aconites these days, do you? When I was a little girl in Yorkshire I remember peering into the rectory grounds to see the hundreds of the little yellow lamps running wild, making a golden carpet. But the old rectory has been bulldozed down long ago and replaced by a smart housing estate with not an aconite in sight. There are lots of snowdrops though, planted by proud owners of smart gardens.

Snowdrops race after aconites in the early battle for light and space and are now drifting along everyone's paths and borders. We used to have huge clumps of them flowering on the roadside. Little children often came to pick them and made posies to take home.

However, the snowdrops lining our roadside are dying out. I don't think that this is because little children are picking them but maybe because of the increasing traffic on our lanes.

The snowdrops, however, like all wildlife will do anything to survive and they have crept under the hedge and through into our orchard. So now we have drifts of their white heads defiantly flowering under the fruit trees. Waking worker bees will soon welcome being able to drink their nectar.

One warm morning last week I saw a yawning bumble bee queen grateful for very early nectar from our aconites. Unwittingly she took pollen from flower to flower so that soon there will be little purses of black seeds. The seeds could eventually settle on the ground and if they race the new choking spring hedgerow plants, they can grow into aconite seedlings. I will welcome them because aconites, precariously clinging to their place as first flowerers, seem to be losing the race.

Where did my aconites come from then? Well, I will tell you a secret I have not told anyone before. Years ago, my grandmother, on seeing the bulldozer in the rectory grounds, waited for dusk. Then she took a paper bag and a trowel and, in the shadow of the great trees, dug up some aconite tubers. The flowers had died back already and the round lobed leaves were strong. She crept away with her loot. I suppose you could say that she stole them but she also saved them. She planted them in her own garden and the next year they flowered. Then they seeded and the seedlings spread and made another golden carpet. The following year my grandmother gave me some little black seeds in a paper bag.

I sowed my seeds under our hedge and here they are now. The 'Grandchildren' of stolen aconites from a Yorkshire rectory garden are growing here in Shropshire.

The bleary-eyed bumble bee I saw last week didn't mind at all where they came from or even if they were stolen goods. She just seized the opportunity to feed, nothing else mattered to her. Wildlife will stop at nothing to win the survival stakes.

March
The unwelcome wasp

Have you noticed that birds are already looking for suitable places to nest? I have seen blue tits going in and out of our bird box opposite the kitchen window.

At the bottom of our garden I have a little summer house. It is beyond the woodland and away from it all. A place to read or listen to the radio or just to look out and soak up the sun and watch the comings and goings of birds. I had an idea a few years ago, that I could put up a glass sided nest box and if there was a rectangle cut out of my summer house wall I could see the birds and watch their antics. It was such a simple idea with no special equipment needed. I even made a curtain to give the birds privacy. What could go wrong? Well, everything went wrong because no birds have ever nested there.

Perhaps they don't like the position, perhaps they don't like the glass or even my curtain. Whatever the reason, they don't nest there. I have stopped looking until this week. I went to check, just on the off chance.

I pulled the curtain back and it was full – of something. At first, I could not quite make it out. It must be a bird's nest – it was flaked grey – the long-tailed tit makes nests from grey lichens. I looked closer and it was a nest but not made by a bird. It is a wasps' nest.

Domed and made to fit, there are layers and layers of a soft papery material in grey, cream and white. In the warm weather, you have probably heard wasps rasping a wooden fence or in my case our back door that needs painting. The wasps chew these slivers of wood to make the walls of their nest.

Last spring a queen wasp must have found my empty and dry bird box, and could not believe her luck. She had found the ideal spot to lay her eggs which would hatch into workers.

This old nest is abandoned now and all the wasps are dead apart from young fertilised queens who are not here. They are hidden elsewhere in cracks and crevices until the warm spring. The process starts again soon, so watch out, you might have the beginning of a nest in your garage or porch.

Wasps should be our friends – they are sociable and work together like honey bees. They also eat garden pests. But we do not like wasps. They should be welcome but they are not and that's because they sting.

Sometimes in the summer we accidentally come across a wasps' nest on Oak Meadow in our sandy soil. The wasps chase us and get in our hair and our clothes. Then they sting. But we must not run into the house because this brings the wasps indoors and they will sting everyone else. We must hit our heads hard to kill the stingers in our hair. Then we must take our clothes off and check that we are free of wasps before we come indoors.

So, if you visit us don't be surprised if you see a scantily clad person frantically hitting her head. Don't laugh, it could be your turn next!

March
The hungry heron

The frogs are back. I have not been there to look yet but I know, without even going over the wet grass to the pond in the corner of Oak Meadow. I sit here in our house and look through the window across the field and I know. It's a mystery until you know, then it's obvious.

We have had the spring equinox, equal day equal night, and can look forward to longer days. The pond in the corner of Oak Meadow has filled with water – it has taken all winter for the water to run in from the fields and now it is February full. But watch out! March, the god of war with his spear, tells that it is not all over yet. March can bring more heavy rain.

Little Alfie, came to stay this week. We played the usual endless Hide and Seek then the eternal Treasure Hunt – children never get tired of the old games especially when internet connection is not fast enough. The Treasure Hunt is the best and it goes like this – little pieces of paper are cut up and clues put on each one. The papers are hidden all over the garden. Alfie was writing the clues this year 'all gone' wrote Alfie (now 6 and doing well at school). What did he mean all gone? It was a mystery – what could have gone? The answer had to be in the garden, those are the rules. So, we hunted round but found nothing – well we wouldn't would we if they had all gone? Alfie would not tell. He won, we lost. But still he would not tell.

I gave up and took Alfie across Oak Meadow and told him how I knew the frogs were back now it is

17

spring. The clue was the heron flying over and I saw it land on the bank of the pond and then stand frozen like a statue on long legs. He was looking for frogs to eat and the heron won't come to our field pond until the frogs arrive. The heron chicks have hatched in the tall tree nests at the local heronry and I imagine that the parents come as far as our pond to get food. They eat four times as much food when they are feeding their young so they must go looking for creatures. They eat fish, frogs, young birds and small mammals like mice. They spear them with their long, pointed beaks. Disturbed by us, our heron flew to the home-made duck pond but he didn't stay long was nothing to eat for him there.

Alfie showed us the answer to his clue, before he left. He took us to our garden ornamental pool which we have carefully planted with marginal plants and lilies. They are only just beginning to show fresh shoots. Normally swimming in and out of the plants are ten big healthy goldfish. They have weathered the winter hardly moving at the bottom of the pond and this month have begun to be livelier. But as we looked, I suddenly knew what Alfie meant. They had indeed 'all gone'.

I wonder who could have taken them?

April
The blackbirds' eggs

Down a cinder path from our back door there is a little old brick shed and inside there used to be a lavatory. Some people might remember earth closets, as I do. There was a scrubbed pine seat with a hole in. If you had the superior model there were two holes. Two of you could sit side by side.

The seat has long gone and the little closet is now called a 'potting shed' in memory of its original purpose. Here we sow our seeds in trays and root our cuttings in plant pots on a work surface put up for the purpose. The door, almost off its rusty hinges, is slumped permanently open. The brick walls still show some original white paint and there is a rusty nail sticking out which would have held cut up squares of newspaper (you know what for). The nail now holds seed packets.

Very early last month two blackbirds started to nest in our conifer hedge. I saw the female, much duller than the male, carrying dried grass, small twigs and moss. She worked for several days while her male counterpart flew about keeping guard. I don't know if she laid eggs there but after a while both birds disappeared. There are lots of predators of birds' eggs and young.

I didn't look for the nest because I remember once I found a robins' nest and have regretted it ever since. I saw the robins taking hay into the undergrowth. After two weeks, I saw them taking insects and I began to search. It wasn't long before I found the nest. I held my breath as I watched four little skinny heads with black down sticking up on top. At my approach, they simultaneously opened their big mouths and I watched massive orange gapes waiting for food. Then I heard the parent 'tick, tick' warning me to go and so I crept away. I noticed I had trampled the soft herbage leading to the nest. I had left a clear trail showing the way to the nest.

It wasn't long before the robins' 'tick, tick' could be heard again and this time it was accompanied by the cackle of a magpie. I watched horrified as the magpie made a dive into the undergrowth. I ran shouting and clapping but I was too late. The magpie had raided the robins' nest.

I decided there and then that I would never approach a bird nest ever again. But I had reckoned without our blackbirds. At least I imagine it is the same pair because not long after they abandoned the conifer, the female was going backwards and forwards taking dried grass into our potting shed. And all the while the male with his shiny black coat and bright yellow beak kept guard.

Now, when we go to pot up plants or sow seeds there on a shelf, amongst tumbling plastic pots, cobwebs and old wicker baskets, is a blackbirds' nest. They sit and watch our comings and goings and we can't help seeing them. Sometimes the female is sitting and sometimes it's the male. Sometimes they leave for a break and there, just in front of us, are four beautiful blue smudged eggs. I expect they will hatch any time now.

April
The sweet cowslips

I remember cowslips flowering in April when I was young. They grew on the side of our railway line. Every day huge steam trains thundered through on their way to the seaside town, then back again at night taking trippers home.

Along the railway were swathes of unattended land, rather like the side of the motorway these days. Between the taut wire fencing and the rail lines there frolicked all sorts of plants and animals. They were a tough breed because every now and again a burning coal or a spark fell from the train and everything caught fire. The smouldering flames burnt fast and uncontrolled, racing with the train. Things had to be strong to survive there. The cowslips somehow escaped burning and every April their flowers came out in profusion, hanging demurely like a bunch of keys. They carpeted huge areas of our line side.

At that time of year two men came on a little rail buggy with no roof. It was hand powered by them both. They scooted along the rails standing up and pushing a bar in turn like Laurel and Hardy. They were dressed in big navy trousers with heavy coats and railway issue hats to match.

They came to check the nuts and bolts on the line. We saw them going into a nearby wooden cabin with no windows. The shed was padlocked but they had a huge bunch of keys and one key fitted the lock to their cabin. They made a little garden outside and at lunch time they sat out on wooden chairs in the sun, drinking their tea from mugs. Sometimes they fell asleep after their drink. Then they worked again until nightfall when they locked the cabin and jumped on their little buggy and set off back home.

Sometimes I saw them picking huge bunches of cowslips and taking them into the cabin. I picked the cowslips too and took them home to put on our table in a jam-jar. Sometimes I pulled the little florets from their green casement and sucked the narrow tube at the base. I could taste the nectar and in the days when sweets were rationed that was a seductive taste.

The wild cowslip flowers are out now on Oak Meadow. These are the true wild cowslips with little pale petals peeping out from a pale green tube. They are rare to find in a field these days, probably because of our modern farming but you can still see them growing wild in some hidden places in Shropshire and occasionally on motorway embankments.

Twenty years ago, I found one little plant on the banks of the pond in the corner. Now there is a whole sweep of cowslips. We have so many that last year we picked a bucket full and made cowslip wine. It is excellent and has a sweet, nectary taste.

Now telling you all this, has made me wonder what the men were doing with all the cowslips they picked. I am also wondering if it really was tea in their mugs!

May
The bird tree

As I write this I keep stopping to stare out of the kitchen window. Not that we have a fantastic view but there is something happening there that I think will interest you.

Many years ago, I took a cutting from a friend's bay tree because, you will know, bay trees are very expensive. I set about growing the cutting and after many years (about 25) I had my very own mop head bay tree. Then it started growing shoots, I let them grow and clipped a second smaller mop on the top of the first one.

About a month ago a song thrush started bringing dried grass and moss and built a nest in the lower mop. I saw her bring a beak full of mud from our gateway to line the nest. She was very careful and she waited on the fence first, then onto a nearby stone and then up and under the ball, when she was sure no one was watching. But I was watching from our kitchen window. After a few days, the male sat on the fence to sing. He sang all his songs twice 'lest you should think he never could recapture the first fine careless rapture'. The female was sitting on the eggs. Then the chicks hatched and both birds have been going backwards and forwards with food. Everywhere I go now, I see broken snail shells on the thrush 'anvil'. Near a stone or a concrete path, the thrush holds a snail in its beak and bangs it on the hard surface to get to the soft inside.

Yesterday the fledglings burst onto our terrace, begging for food and looking strangely gangly and vulnerable.

The song thrush is now on the red list. This means that it is on the danger list and that its numbers have dropped drastically in recent years. It's hard to imagine that we might lose the familiar song thrush with its 'first fine careless rapture'.

We have stopped using slug pellets so that we do not poison slugs and snails and inadvertently kill the thrush but there is not much else we can do, except hope for the best.

You might wonder why I am still staring out of the kitchen window when the baby thrushes have fledged. Well, just after the thrush had settled down to hatch her young, two bullfinches started showing an interest in the top mop on the bay tree. I first saw them hovering like hummingbirds, with their white rumps contrasting with their black tails and heads. The male's breast was a startling strong pink. Before long the female, who is a little duller than her partner, was surreptitiously bringing twigs and there they settled in the second floor above the thrush.

Bullfinches eat fruit tree buds I have seen them eating ours. No wonder fruit tree growers used to trap them until we got worried that they too could be under threat. They are on the amber list already.

I have one red and one amber, so all I need now is to grow a third bay ball on top and hope that common blackbirds nest there. Blackbirds are on the green list, so I could have a full set of traffic lights!

May
The tame robin

Have you got a robin in your garden? I don't know why but robins are very special to us; maybe it's because of their attractive red breast or that they are very brave and sometimes come up to humans for food. I have even heard of robins eating out of people's hands. Perhaps yours does.

I remember watching my mother shaking the table cloth onto our cobbles outside our Yorkshire farmhouse. The robin was always there, almost in the fold of the gingham, as she shook. It was looking for bread crumbs to eat. My mother didn't have time to look though, she had to go quickly to help milk the cows. She used to wear a brown milking coat and later kept it as a souvenir. Eventually I brought it back to Shropshire. Not to wear, but because I could not bear to throw it away. It hangs here, faded and torn, on a rusty hook on our crumbling shed door. We store corn for the hens in our shed and sometimes I see the robin flitting in and out.

We want to help the robin find a nesting place in our garden so we have put up special robin nest boxes. We have even hidden a kettle in a bush because you see pictures in children's books with robins nesting in kettles. But it has all been to no avail – I could not spot where our robin was nesting, until two weeks ago. I went in our old shed to get corn for the hens and out flew the robin in an unusual flurry. I looked at my mother's old milking coat hanging up. There, in the pocket, was a collection of moss, dried grass and feathers. It was the robins' nest.

Soon there were speckled baby robins all over our lawn and the parents were going backwards and forwards in desperation to find food for their young. A favourite place to get creatures is behind the wisteria clinging to our house wall. This year it has been covered with cascading flowers (it's all in the pruning), they attract insects by their sweet smell. The parent robins have been up and down there every day. I sat outside and had my cup of tea and cake and watched.

I remember being told a story, long ago, about how the robin got his red breast. Someone (probably an imp) had tied the sun down with rope so that it could not rise. The world got darker and no one knew what to do. Then the brave robin rose high in the sky until he reached the rope. His breast feathers were singed red by the sun but he bravely pecked until the rope broke and the sun was free and shot up into the sky to shine out.

Today the robin was desperately brave again and came to my garden table when I was there. He was begging for a piece of my cake. He sat on my cup and stared wistfully at me with his head on one side.

At the end of the day, after supper, I cleared the kitchen table and shook the cloth outside. Then there was the robin again, flying in the folds of linen, looking for that very last crumb.

June
The mysterious foxglove

There is deep wizardry about the foxgloves' crowded steeples of pink bells with 'great black bees that swing them,' wrote Shropshire's Mary Webb. The wild spires are pointing skywards from our hedgerows everywhere today.

The foxglove, seemingly, has nothing to do with foxes but more to do with the little folks. Folks' glove, so they say. The fairy folk can make your dreams come true.

The foxglove bells are supposed to be lucky and will grant wishes. I knew this from childhood when we had foxgloves growing under our laburnum tree. They flowered together, purple-pink with bright yellow, it is not everyone's favourite colour combination. But we didn't care about matching colours then, nor did we care about health and safety.

All parts of the foxglove are poisonous and children these days would not be allowed to play with them like I did. We didn't know then that the foxglove produces the powerful chemical digitoxin which acts on the heartbeat. No animal ever eats foxglove because they know that it's dangerous.

One night, I secretly put a foxglove flower on each thumb and made a wish. I knew that you had to go to sleep with the bell petals on, like thimbles. If they were both still on your thumbs in the morning your wish would be granted. It was in the days of sugar rationing and I wished for a bar of Five Boys chocolate. I fell asleep in expectation. I didn't tell anyone what my wish was because that would break the spell. But it didn't matter anyway because the flower bells came off in the night and left behind only soft crushed petals at the bottom of my bed, near my toes.

After all these years I am looking for wild foxgloves in the garden. They stubbornly resist all my efforts to transplant them or to sow their seeds where I want. Instead they pop up, as if by magic, in shady places of their choice. This one is growing just over the hedge with bright yellow buttercups in the field beyond (that colour combination again). I put my thumb in a bell and it is surprisingly strong made of four petals fused into one. I can see a bumble bee fly onto the lip of the lower petal. It follows the round bubble spots which go deep into the tube and disappears down there, drinking nectar. And all the while the big bell clappers, which do not ring but are anthers full of pollen, dust the bee. There is no room for the fat bumble to turn and it must back out. I watch as, pollen covered and hungry for more, it buzzes into another flower. Unwittingly it makes sure we have seeds for next year.

I think I will try making a wish again. I have picked two bells for tonight. What will I wish for? You will want to know. Should I wish for a 'good' election result? No, I think I will go for my childhood idea and wish for a bar of chocolate. I wonder if the 'deep wizardry' will work this time, even though I have just realised that they don't make Five Boys chocolate any more.

With foxglove magic, anything could happen.

June
The baby blackbird

Our song thrush and blackbird have second broods. The thrush is sitting again on four pure blue eggs in the bay tree just below our bedroom window and the blackbird laid eggs again in their nest on a shelf in our potting shed.

They have hatched four young from their first eggs and have now tried again. Both blackbird and thrush sat tight on their nests of hatching eggs.

Then one morning, very early, there was a 'drip, drip dripping' outside our bedroom window. In my dream, I thought that we had water all over the bedroom. But when I woke up in a panic thinking we would be flooded, I realised that it was a 'chick, chick, chick' that I could hear. It was an alarm but it wasn't my bedside alarm clock, it was the scolding call of the blackbird outside. Then I heard the sad cries of the song thrush. Bleary eyed we opened the window and saw that a magpie was raiding the song thrush's nest. The young defenceless nestlings had just hatched. We saw the babies being dragged out and devoured by the magpie. We caught him in the act and we clapped and shouted (sorry neighbours), but he gulped down the last blind hatchling. Then he flew off over Oak Meadow with a cackle.

You probably know that the song thrush is in danger and relies on our gardens for nesting. Suitable hedgerows in fields are scarce and not many nests are successful. Song thrushes are in danger and we want to help. There is not much we can do about magpies but we can help in another way.

Thrushes eat slugs and snails so, to make sure the thrush is not poisoned, a lot of people like us have stopped using the normal slug pellets. Instead, we often went out at night and picked the slugs and snails off our plants. This was a horrible job and so we have made slug traps.

You will be pleased to know that the potting shed blackbirds fared better than the thrushes. The young hatched safely and soon the parents were going backwards and forwards again with beaks full of worms. They were safe from the magpie who did not dare venture into our potting shed, especially when we were there. Yesterday the baby blackbirds fledged and took their first frantic flight into our garden. They were on our lawn begging for food from their busy parents. But one fledgling was more hesitant than its brothers and sisters and I caught him trembling in our potting shed on a shelf between a can of cider and a can of lager.

Now it is not what you think. We do not pop into the potting shed for a quick drink. We use the alcohol to make traps for the slugs (honestly). We fill a jar and half bury it. The slugs can't resist a sip or two, then they fall in.

The good news is that the reluctant baby blackbird eventually left the safety of alcohol cans and flew off. Also, the thrush has built a new nest in a bush just outside our front door. I am hoping that the magpies dare not come near this time. Now I will drink to that!

July
The invasion of bees

One day I heard a loud noise like a low flying helicopter in the field called Goose Bottom and I rushed over to see what was happening. There was a huge black cloud moving towards our garden. We were being invaded.

We have a beehive in that field, it not ours it belongs to some beekeepers who live in town. The bees pollinate our fruit trees. The bees get nectar and the beekeepers get honey – it was a simple plan. Everyone benefits.

I have a little chair near the hive where I go and sit and watch the bees bringing nectar to make honey and carrying pollen on their knees. The tall grass almost hides my view and the hay rattle flower heads are full of seeds. In and out go the bees with not a moment to lose, they must get their winter stores of honey built up. Hidden deep in the hive is the queen controlling events.

And all the while the swallows dip and dive overhead catching flies.

Then I noticed that the bees had started to cover the front of the hive. Soon the whole surface was a crawling, fascinating mass. Then for no reason that I could see one started to buzz round me 'buzz off' I said waving my hand to swat her but she didn't go. I got up and walked briskly away – she followed and I could hear her very close to my face. Now let me tell you from experience you cannot outrun an angry bee – she stung me. I went in the house and that was when I heard the helicopter noise.

It was a spectacular sight with dark black dots moving at random over the field eclipsing the sky. The bees had formed a cloud, like smoke from a fire that hung and buzzed. I watched from a safe distance as they rose and sank in unison, following the queen in a whirling mass. They tried my chair for size but rejected it and eventually settled on our pear tree.

And there grew a giant black pear, dwarfing the little green ones already on the tree. The noise stopped and I knew that scout bees would be out looking for a suitable place for the queen to lay her eggs and start another colony. Everything was quiet now. The old hive would have a new queen growing and she would have the workers that had been left behind. But I was in a bit of a panic. What do you do with a swarm of bees? Having bees in Goose Bottom is not as simple as I thought.

'A swarm of bees in July is not worth a fly,' according to the old saying. No one wants a swarm in July.

Well, that is not quite true because I phoned our beekeepers and they came and tapped the branch so the giant pear of bees fell into a waiting basket.

Now we have two hives and although the new bees will need help with winter food as they have no store – all is well. I feel like the bee's knees for being part of the successful drama.

Bees are on the decline and so we do want a swarm of bees, even in July, and the swallows want the fly.

July
The ugly caterpillar

I think that I have found the world's worst looking creature eating willow herb in Oak Meadow. July is the month for caterpillars and this one looks fearful. Its skin is wrinkly and grey like an elephant and its 'eyes' are menacing and glaring.

Whether you know it or not insect eggs of all kinds have already been laid secretly in our gardens and fields. They are hatching out now into tiny caterpillars. They will eat your plant leaves and grow bigger and fatter. Look out for holes in the leaves of your flower plants and vegetables. Sometimes all that is left is the stalk.

If you are lucky (or unlucky depending on your point of view) you could see this fearsome creature as I did. When I tried to touch it, huge eyes seemed to blow up and swell from nowhere and at its tail end it had a sharp looking point like a sting. I would think it was trying to frighten its enemies and stop it from being eaten; it certainly frightened me when I first saw one.

Years ago, when I had a young family I found a creature like this in my overgrown garden. I had just moved there and the garden was a mess but that did not bother me because the house was nice. I say the weeds didn't bother me but that was before I saw this creature one night when I went out to collect the washing. It had eyes as big as saucers (well nearly) and a 'sting' that looked fearsome. I trod on it firmly and squashed it before it could hurt the children. Too late, I discovered that it wouldn't hurt anyone. It was a caterpillar looking for a place to pupate and not a person to hurt.

The next time I saw one I put it in an insect cage with mesh on the top so it could 'breathe' and I gave it leaves and some soil. It burrowed a little way down and spun a silken cocoon and changed into a chrysalis. I left it on the shelf in the utility room. Then one day in spring I noticed a fluttering and there was a beautiful elephant hawk moth. It was bright pink mixed with lime green. I let it out that night onto the willow herb at the bottom of the garden.

Rosebay willow herb is called fireweed because it grows on wasteland often after there has been a fire. I remember fireweed growing in Hull, which is near where I used to live. Hull was an important port and was bombed mercilessly in WW11. I used to walk in the rubble of people's houses with fireweed defiantly waving purple flowers on stems covered in leaves. I didn't see any elephant hawk moths or their caterpillars though. I don't think they had ventured that far north.

The elephant hawk moth lives in Shropshire so look out for the beautiful bright pink and green moths drinking nectar in the evening from flowers. The moths will die soon, they only live about a month, but the caterpillars will be getting fat and be out to scare you if you get too near. Don't be deceived though as I was once, they will not harm you.

August
The devil's dragonfly

I don't know if you have noticed that the screaming has stopped in our towns. What the devil has been going on? There has been screaming in town during the day for that last few months, it started in May but suddenly it has gone. No more screaming around the town.

But there has been screaming in our garden today when my visitor, little Alfie, ran away from a monster which seemed to be chasing him. He thought that it had a big sting and it made a strange whirring sound as it zoomed around at top speed.

It was a dragonfly and it was not chasing little Alfie, it was chasing a bee. I told him there was no need to be frightened but I didn't tell him that dragonflies used to be called The Devil's Darning Needle, he wouldn't know what a darning needle is. Who darns these days? If you wear a hole in your sock you simply buy a new pair from the shop.

Also, when I was young I heard that dragonflies fly into your bedroom at night and look for naughty children and then using their darning needle body they stitch up boys' mouths. I didn't tell Alfie this either but I did tell him what I saw this morning.

If you have a pond in your garden you could see it too. You will have to get up quite early when the sun has just risen. This morning that is what I did — and when I arrived at our little pond I saw that in the night a black demon-like creature had climbed a reed growing from the water and was holding on fiercely with its strong legs.

Then something unbelievable happened, the skin started to split and gradually a colourless dragonfly emerged – it looked so fragile and its legs were floppy, it would surely fall into the murky pond water and die. I held my breath but the dragonfly was attached to a little piece of white thread, just like a climber held on by a rope. It was safe and it pulled itself out of its old skin and unfolded.

The sun was shining and its wings opened and grew as I watched. After about an hour the dragonfly turned green and it was all pumped up and flew away.

The ugly creature which had lived for years in our little pond had changed into a beautiful dragonfly, a magical metamorphosis. But dragonflies don't live long and die after laying their eggs. They will soon be gone.

The swifts have gone already, they laid their eggs high up in the buildings around town and now they have all flown back to Africa. It was the swifts that were screaming around town. People used to be frightened of them and called them Devil's Birds. But they, like dragonflies, are not dangerous and there is no need to be frightened.

Swifts and dragonflies are declining and it could be climate change or loss of habitat – now that is something that really frightens me, you can't just go shopping and buy new ones like you can socks.

I must go and tell little Alfie this, because I can see that, reassured about the dragonfly, he is now chasing it and having the devil of a time.

August
The spotted fly catcher

A farmer friend once told me about this little bird he had seen nesting in his clematis surrounding his front porch.

'It's just a little brown bird with a speckled head,' he said, 'but it flies off and comes back to the same place every time. It's as if it is fastened to a branch by a piece of elastic.'

Many years later we have that little bird in our garden – well not the same one but it fits the description exactly. It is a spotted flycatcher and if you have one in your garden you are very lucky indeed. It is on the red list because it's a bird that is now rare in Britain.

About three weeks ago, I saw a pair of birds going backwards and forwards in our woodland glade. I thought no more about it – just little brown birds. But then one day my husband heard a loud 'tac, tac' and saw the two little brown birds shouting and flapping their wings at a grey squirrel running up the silver birch tree trunk. They were dive bombing the squirrel and making such a noise so that eventually he gave up and went over to the yew tree. It took us ages to find the nest with our binoculars. It's about ten feet off the ground, hidden against the tree trunk, in amongst ivy leaves.

We set up the telescope at a distance and arranged two chairs one behind the other. The person on the front seat has the premier view of the nest through the telescope on a tripod. The person on the back seat must use the binoculars which are not as good because they do not magnify as well. After an agreed time, we swap seats. Once, when I had the ringside seat, I saw the male feed the female, on the nest, with a big bluebottle fly.

The female sat all day and all night for two weeks and the male caught insects to give to her. He does not go looking for insects in the ground or on leaves, he just sits there on a branch and waits. Woe betide any fly, big or small, that happens to pass by. The flycatcher swoops and catches his prey mid-air with a snap of his beak, then he returns to his perch. It is just like my farmer friend described; it really does look as if the flycatcher is attached by an elastic thread to the branch. Do you remember those toys with a ping pong ball stapled to a bat with elastic thread? The ball always bounced back, just like the flycatcher.

The eggs have hatched now and both birds are feeding the babies. I can see the young stretch their scrawny necks and reach for a juicy fly. I saw a parent take a white faecal sac out of the nest, like a poo in a plastic bag. I saw her swallow it, I hope she spat it out later!

The fledglings must grow fast because they need to get ready for a long journey. In four weeks, they will all fly to Africa and if we are lucky the imaginary elastic thread will pull them back here next year.

I have booked the ringside seat already.

September
The bumble bee

Everything is not what it seems on Oak Meadow. There is still the echo of the soft sound of summer as the bumble bees go from flower to flower, but don't be deceived. The bumbles will not be taking food back to their nests – which are empty now and beginning to rot.

Bumble bees are massed all over Oak Meadow visiting the startling blue field scabious flowers. Last week I watched them and once they found a good nectar source, they visited over and over again in their bid to survive.

But the big bees that I saw going from flower to flower were not workers collecting pollen and nectar to feed their grubs or to store food for the winter like honey bees do. These were the new queens and some drones. And you might be surprised to know that the workers and the old queens are all dead or dying.

The new queens must feed as quickly as they can and get fatter and fatter. They must then mate. The males will not survive the winter.

So, if you see a bumble bee today it will be a young queen she will be feeding up to a heavy weight (for a bumble bee) and then she must hibernate. Already the big bumbles that have reached a good weight have gone underground.

Soon they will all be underground. Only the young queens survive the winter and to do this they dig holes in the soil.

But the hole the queen digs is only a few centimetres down and what if it freezes? Her cells would freeze too and she would die. But all is not what you would think. A bumblebee has a sort of antifreeze in its cells and so can bear very low temperatures indeed and still survive the winter. If it freezes outside she will not die, her antifreeze stops her cells going solid.

Strawberries do not have antifreeze though and my cousin, in Yorkshire, has to rely on heated greenhouses to stop his crop spoiling in the frost. He sells strawberries to supermarkets out of season because we want to eat strawberries at all times, even in the winter. He invited me to see how it worked. I expected to see lots of people with little brushes pollinating the flowers but instead there were bumble bees flying all over the greenhouse. And in various places around the greenhouse there were little cardboard boxes with holes in for the bees to use as hives. I was amazed.

'You are out of date,' my cousin laughed. Nowadays commercial growers all buy bumble bees to pollinate their greenhouse strawberries. Bumble bees work longer hours than the honey bees and at lower temperatures. They are also much better at pollinating than honey bees because they carry much more pollen and give the strawberries a plump round shape. If you grow strawberries, have you sometimes noticed an odd shaped one, dented in on one side? Well, that means that a bumble bee has not visited.

And have you heard that research has supposed to have proved that theoretically bumble bees cannot fly because of their weight? Surely, they cannot defy science? Well, I could believe anything of the super bumble bees, they are not as bumbling as they seem.

September
The jumping grasshopper

When did you last hear a grasshopper? When did you see one jumping? I imagine that you can remember them from childhood when they seemed to be on every little piece of spare land. They were the sound of long hot summer days and hay meadows.

These days I don't often hear grasshoppers, but walking through Oak Meadow today in the long grass there was an unmistakable chirping. And that is not all because as I walked along the path I could see them jumping ahead of me. At first, I think that I am kicking up small pieces of grass on either side. If I stop, they stop, I bend down and I can see them – about an inch long staying dead still until I move then they jump again. I can see them warming themselves on the sunny side of the path. There are many different types and mine is the common green grasshopper with thin white lines curving on its back.

I used to be able to catch them in my hands when I was young. My sisters and cousins played – 'Whose grasshopper can jump the highest?' You had to hold it and on the word 'now,' you let it go and watched it jump. It was very hard to judge who had won the competition. But we soon went off to catch more. We kept them as pets in match boxes, but I expect they jumped out as soon as we peeped in.

I tried to catch one in my hands today but I had no luck they are too quick for me now. Grasshoppers can leap up about 10 times their own height and they look as if they have been fired from a catapult. They certainly know how to jump, seemingly without effort.

We knew how to jump too. We could jump gates and ditches. We could jump on and off hay stacks and bounce on rolled wire netting until we were almost flying with our arms in the air. We jumped for joy.

But when I went to High School, I was told that I was not jumping properly. I had to learn all over again. We had a spring board to jump a 'horse' and rows of hurdles to scale, with our legs moving in a set way and our arms in another way. I was at the bottom of the class for jumping even though I had jumped all my life. I must say that when I was not at school I still jumped in the way I had always jumped.

And here the grasshoppers are still jumping in the way they have always done with their strong muscular back legs suddenly pushing up from the ground.

Today the males are chirping hopefully to the females and showing off to them. They make their noise in an unusual way – by rubbing their legs against their wings. There are pegs on the legs like a comb which makes the strange 'song'. Their eggs are already safely hidden in the soil and hopefully they will hatch in the spring. The adults will die soon and we will not hear the chirping nor see the jumping for joy again until next summer.

October
The baby owl

You know, of course, that owls do not call twit-twoo. They sometimes shout 'twit' and sometimes 'twoo'. They are the separate calls of the tawny owl.

The 'twit' call sounds more like a sharp 'ke-wick'. But the shout 'twit' is not as rude as it sounds, to an owl it is a friendly contact between owls, it is comforting like the tune on your mobile when a friend is ringing for a chat.

'Hello I'm here,' one calls and another will call back.

You can hear them at night in the spring calling 'twit' to each other as they start laying eggs and incubating, then feeding their babies.

Thinking of baby owls, reminds me of the time when I was walking in a Shropshire woodland, not far from here, I found a helpless, baby tawny owl on the ground. It had been raining and the baby was very wet. I picked him up carefully and felt its soft young down and was surprised that my fingers sank through layers of feathers. Its tiny bony skeleton was deeply embedded in its fluffed-out shape. Its eyes were round and black and frightened. I know that you should not touch a baby bird – its parents always know where it is and will visit to feed. But I couldn't put him back in a puddle, could I? He must have fallen off a branch, I thought. Baby owls come out of their nest about a week before they are ready to fly. But then sadly, this little owl must have lost his footing and crashed into a puddle

He felt so soggy and was not moving at all but I could feel is little heart pounding under my fingers. What could I do? In the end I reached up and set him carefully on the highest branch I could reach. I took a photo of him and then I quietly tiptoed away. After three sunny days I went back, with my own heart pounding, hoping all was well. I found that my baby owl had sheltered in tree trunk ivy. He turned his head and gave me a beady stare. He was going to be alright and I think I had saved him.

Last night at home I heard the 'twoo' call of a tawny owl coming from our ivy-covered ash tree. It is quite a ghostly sound – 'whoo-oo'.

I hope my baby owl is fully grown now and hooting 'whoo-oo' into the night telling other owls 'go elsewhere this is my place'. He will shout into the darkness and even tell his own young to go away and find a place of their own, because he is now thinking of his next year's eggs and babies.

I have read recently about Eric Hosking, the famous photographer. Apparently when he was trying to photograph a tawny owl he was struck in the face by the adult's claws. His eye became infected and he had to have it taken out. Mind you afterwards he wrote a book called 'An eye for a bird' and bravely went back to take more owl photographs.

It's a good job that I didn't know all this when I was rescuing my baby owl.

October
The clever hedgehog

One day a friend handed my husband a bundle wrapped in a towel hoping that he would know what to do. There was a little blue hedgehog inside.

Don't worry if you have never heard of a blue hedgehog, it is not a new species. This one was blue because it was covered in blue preservative paint, the friend had been painting a garden fence and the hedgehog must have been squeezing underneath and managed to cover its back with the paint.

Do you remember that Pam Ayres wrote a poem about hedgehogs? She was bemoaning the fact that they were dim. Why did she write this? Well, she said that it was because when they were travelling across a road at night (they are nocturnal) they did not run when they saw some car headlights coming towards them. A hedgehog's instinct, in time of danger, is to roll into a tight ball. So instead of arriving safely on the other side, they got killed on the road and that was where we used to see most of our hedgehogs. As Pam Ayres put it in her poem they ended up squashed and flat and dead.

Even though our blue little hedgehog was not dead he was very poorly. He must have breathed in the preservative fumes as they were quite pungent and he was even too weak to roll into a ball. It was a good job he did not curl up though because we needed to clean him. We put gardening gloves on and gently wiped some of the paint off using warm water and soap. We put him in an unused rabbit cage and fed him hedgehog food, from the pet shop, to fatten him up. After about a month he seemed fully recovered (if a little blue) and we let him go. He ran off into a pile of old leaves without a backward glance. At least he ran in the opposite direction from the road so he wouldn't get run over.

When I think about it I can't even remember when I last saw a hedgehog squashed and flat on the road can you? The fact is there are not many hedgehogs around to get under our cars these days. It is quite a few years since Pam Ayres wrote her poem and she thought that if we kept on running them over they would become extinct — well they very nearly have become extinct but I don't think it is because we have run them all over. I think it must be because they can't find enough to eat or enough places to hibernate in the winter. So, the advice is to be a bit careless in our gardens and leave twigs and leaf litter around in corners.

We have a very 'rubbishy' garden and we see hedgehogs here every year in the autumn.

At night for the last few weeks a hedgehog has been coming up to our back door to feed and in remembrance of the little blue one we have bought a blue dish. Also, in the hopes that our hedgehog is not stupid, we bought one with HEDGEHOG written on it. Maybe he can read and is not as dim as Pam Ayres thought! Perhaps that is why he is still alive.

November
The thieving rat

Now the darker days are here, I have heard some noises in our loft. Sometimes, I hear sparrows in the spring and summer, pushing under the eaves bringing nesting material or food for their young. But it is autumn now and birds should not be moving about in the loft. Also, the noise is different, it is a loud scratching.

We have two brown hens scratching about in a pen outside. They regularly lay eggs in their hut but recently the eggs disappeared and we had no breakfast. I know that hens stop laying when the days get shorter but usually it is more gradual than this.

"Are they laying away?" asked my Shropshire farmer friend. I searched around their pen but there was no long grass in which to hide a nest full of eggs. It was a mystery.

A mystery that is, until I found a long trail leading from under the water butt to the hen hut. It must be rats. Rats eat hens' eggs, but there were no signs of broken eggs, no egg shells and no yolk spillage. The rats were somehow carrying our eggs away.

Unwelcome visitors are a fact of country life. In the 'good old days' you rang the Council and the rat man, who was later called a rodent inspector, came and sorted it out, no questions asked. Nowadays you can identify your unwelcome visitor on-line, it tells you the signs to look out for. You click on the pest of your choice and book a 'treatment technician'. I decided to go to the friendly Hub at our Library. I waited behind the transparent screen, which is not sound proof and you can hear what people say. When it was my turn I whispered that I needed help. I booked and paid but suddenly felt that it was all so clinical and at the heart of it was a little creature.

If you don't like rats you may not like this but I am beginning to feel sorry for the rats. Do you remember the lovely Ratty, in Wind in the Willows? He is, correctly speaking, a water vole but never mind. We all like Ratty – he is relaxed and loves sailing about in a little boat on the river. He is kind to the helpless Moley and even tried to train the foolish Toady. Ratty was a good creature and I know someone who used to keep a pet rat in his pocket because it was so tame and they liked each other.

However, I did not cancel the technician and our hen's eggs are now there every day. The noise in the loft has gone, but we found out later that a squirrel, coming in through a missing slate, had made a nest. I was relieved that rats had not been in the house.

One part of the mystery remains though, how did the rats carry our eggs off to their burrow? My farmer friend explained that one rat lies on his back and hugs the egg to his stomach with his legs, then another rat grasps his tail and pulls him along.

I am not quite sure about this explanation of how rats carry eggs away. Do you think the farmer was telling me a tale?

November
Fairy-tale fungi

Who lives in a house like this? I don't expect that that Loyd Grossman, who showed us how the rich and famous live, would be interested but I have found these pink topped little structures under our rhododendron bush.

They are called fly agaric and are so welcome on our 'no sun' No-vember day which has no creatures and no flowers for me to write about.

My childhood picture books, show golden haired fairies peeping out of similar pink topped toadstool cottages waiting to make your wishes to come true. So, I think that I can safely say that magical fairies live in a house like this.

You will remember Alice in Wonderland found a magic mushroom with a caterpillar sitting on the top of it smoking a hookah. She was worried about her size and was told by the caterpillar to eat some of the mushroom, 'one side will make you grow taller and the other side will make you grow shorter.' I could do with being a bit taller but eating all sides has made no difference to me.

When I was a child we were never short of fungi, they were everywhere – those you could play with and those you could eat. We knew the difference then, in those days, we had a wisdom which those of you who grew up in the countryside would also have.

What I didn't know is that technically there is no difference between a toadstool and a mushroom. I always thought that you could eat mushrooms, but not toadstools which were poisonous. Well, apparently, not, they are all from the same family.

Every morning, in autumn, we ran out into our pasture to pick horse mushrooms. They were very big and white on the top with light brown gills underneath. If the gills were chocolate brown they were ripe and producing spores and it was too late to eat them. We only needed one or two for breakfast for the whole family. They fried up to a delicious brown mass oozing a gravy and was perfect with our hens' eggs.

We knew that the puff balls we found were for playing with. It was obvious really, they were khaki brown and were the size and shape of a football. If we came across one in the long grass, we naturally kicked it ragged and we could see the spores dusting out all over making sure we would have more fun next year.

When I came to live in Shropshire we cycled down the lane and, leaning our bikes against an oak tree still clinging to crinkled leaves, we filled our pockets with little white mushrooms, freshly nosed through grass. We go to a supermarket now and you may think that fungi do not feature as much in our lives but the Shropshire Fungus Group will tell you that there are 15,000 types in the UK all living on decaying organic material. If you are interested, you can join a group for a fungal foray. Fungi are still everywhere but fairies, to grant your wishes, may be harder to find.

I expect you know that fungi cause athlete's foot. Also, the truffles, for the rich and famous at The London Savoy Grill, are fungi. Take your pick, then make a wish!

December
The wonderful woodpecker

Ever felt that you are banging your head against a brick wall? Spare a thought for the woodpecker with his 'nose of steel...' banging his head against a wall and 'cannot even feel'. Ted Hughes wrote these words in his Woodpecker poem.

My sister's friend knew Ted Hughes when he was in the RAF in a village in Yorkshire where I was born. He wrote some poems in her school book which she kept for 50 years, and recently realised that they might valuable. Was one of the poems was his woodpecker poem?

I don't remember seeing woodpeckers when I was young in Yorkshire but, here in Shropshire, the great spotted woodpecker has been in a field called Ash Patch where there is woodland. All summer he swooped over the garden and clung to trees. If he saw me, he hid round the other side of the trunk and left only his toes visible, two pointing to the front and two pointing backwards. I saw him digging insects out of rough bark and catching them with his long sticky tongue. I also heard him drumming. Apparently, woodpeckers tap 12,000 times a day (who's counting?). They drum with such a force that it is the equivalent of hitting a wall with your head at 20mph, they certainly need their strong skull separated from the beak by shock absorbing pads.

Why isn't this intriguing great spotted woodpecker a favourite bird of ours? He looks so attractive with his sharp black and white stencil pattern and the males have bright red markings on the nape and rump. I have often wondered why they are not on our Christmas cards like our little robins. One reason could be that they eat newly hatched birds and you might have seen and heard them hammering away, trying to get into a blue tit nest box to eat the young. Also, woodpeckers steal our hazel nuts.

I have watched them take nuts from the hazel shrub with their chisel beaks, then wedging them in-between forked branches they hammer the hard covering to get at the soft kernel inside. All we have left is a pile of broken shells at the base of the trunk.

Another thing is, great spotted woodpeckers don't have a song like the robin's wistful winter trill, they only give a sharp alarm call if there is danger. And there is one last thing – why is he called spotted when he is patchy and not spotted at all?

You can see why trying to get the woodpecker picture on Christmas cards would be like banging your head against a brick wall. It would never succeed. It's hard to take them to our hearts and we are not always glad to see them, but we are pleased when the friendly robin comes into our garden.

My sister's friend was pleased too, with her Ted Hughes poems, because once she made it known she had two of his handwritten poems, she had offers to buy them. She sold them to a university in America.

Was one of the newly found poems the woodpecker poem? No, they were both love poems, but at least the famous Ted Hughes did write a poem about the woodpecker and that is more than you can say for the robin.

Have you tried growing mistletoe? It all sounds so easy. Get a seed rub it onto some bark of a tree, stand back and wait. Then on the winter solstice, the shortest day, which is around now, you can go out and pick yourself a bunch of this lucky plant. But it is not as simple as that.

I have tried to grow mistletoe and am about 10 years down the line with it. I went to a market stall – I heard that you needed to use mistletoe from nearby if it was going to be successful – this was from Hereford so I thought I stood a chance. We ran around popping the berries into cracks on trunks of apple, maple and hawthorn trees.

After two years, we had no mistletoe plants, then I heard Bob Flowerdew saying that it was no good using the Christmas berries, you had to wait until they were ripe in March – you keep them on wet sand – I did this and 5 years from the beginning we still had no mistletoe.

I resorted to the internet and bought a kit. We used only apple trees this time, which are apparently the best hosts. I put a seed under a small bough immediately above my head. You squeeze the white berry and a sticky gum comes out surrounding a little seed. I pressed this on the underside of my branch and gently teased out the slime into strands along the bark to make a little net (don't think about it). We 'sowed' more, climbing ladders, pulling branches and reaching up high. Then we forgot about them all.

One day several years later my husband was pruning my apple tree when I heard him shout 'We have mistletoe!' My little branch had borne fruit.

So, we have our very own magic mistletoe. It has now formed a huge ball of light green leaves and it has juicy white translucent berries ready for Christmas.

When we first arrived at this house we planted an orchard using apple and pear saplings. Surprisingly they all blossomed the following year. Then one day in autumn there was a sharp rap on our door and there stood our neighbour, from down the lane, in a smart suit. He was our Parish Councillor.

'Have you planted a pear tree?' he asked briskly.

'Yes,' I answered with a tremble in case there was a by-law against planting pear trees.

'I have had a pear tree for 20 years and it has never borne fruit until this year, so I have your tree as pollinator to thank.' He handed me a basket of pears with a smile.

I have told you this pear story because my mistletoe has fruit so it is a female and as mistletoe is not self-fertile someone nearby must have a male mistletoe. I wonder who you are. You are not too distant because mistletoe is pollinated by little flies and they will not travel far.

I would love to rap on your door and say, 'Have you got mistletoe?' And you would say 'Yes' and then I would hand you a basket of mistletoe with big white berries and you could have as many kisses as there are berries. There is no law against it at Christmas!

*   *   *

The Author

Vicky Turrell is the Nature Correspondent for the Oswestry and Borders Advertizer. She grew up on a farm in Yorkshire and now lives with her husband on a smallholding in Shropshire where wild plants and animals abound.

Vicky enjoys observing how the wildlife survives and she records what she sees, using notes and photographs throughout the year.

'It's Not a Boy!' Vicky's first published book, tells of her early life, growing up on a farm in the 1940s and 50s.